Copyright © 2016 Ye Olde Coloring

Swear Word Coloring Book

All Rights Reserved Worldwide

Ye Olde

Swear Word
Adult Coloring Book

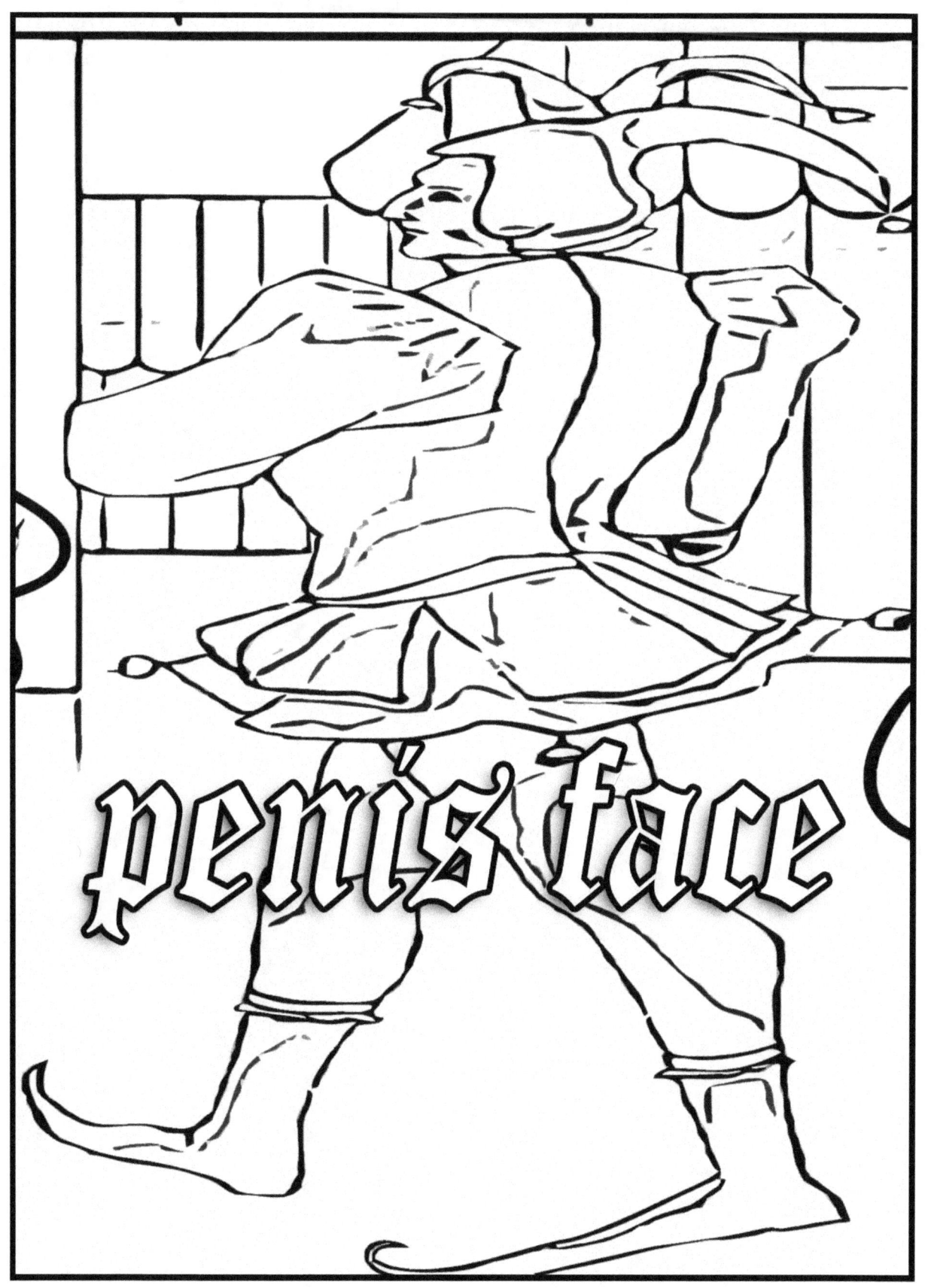

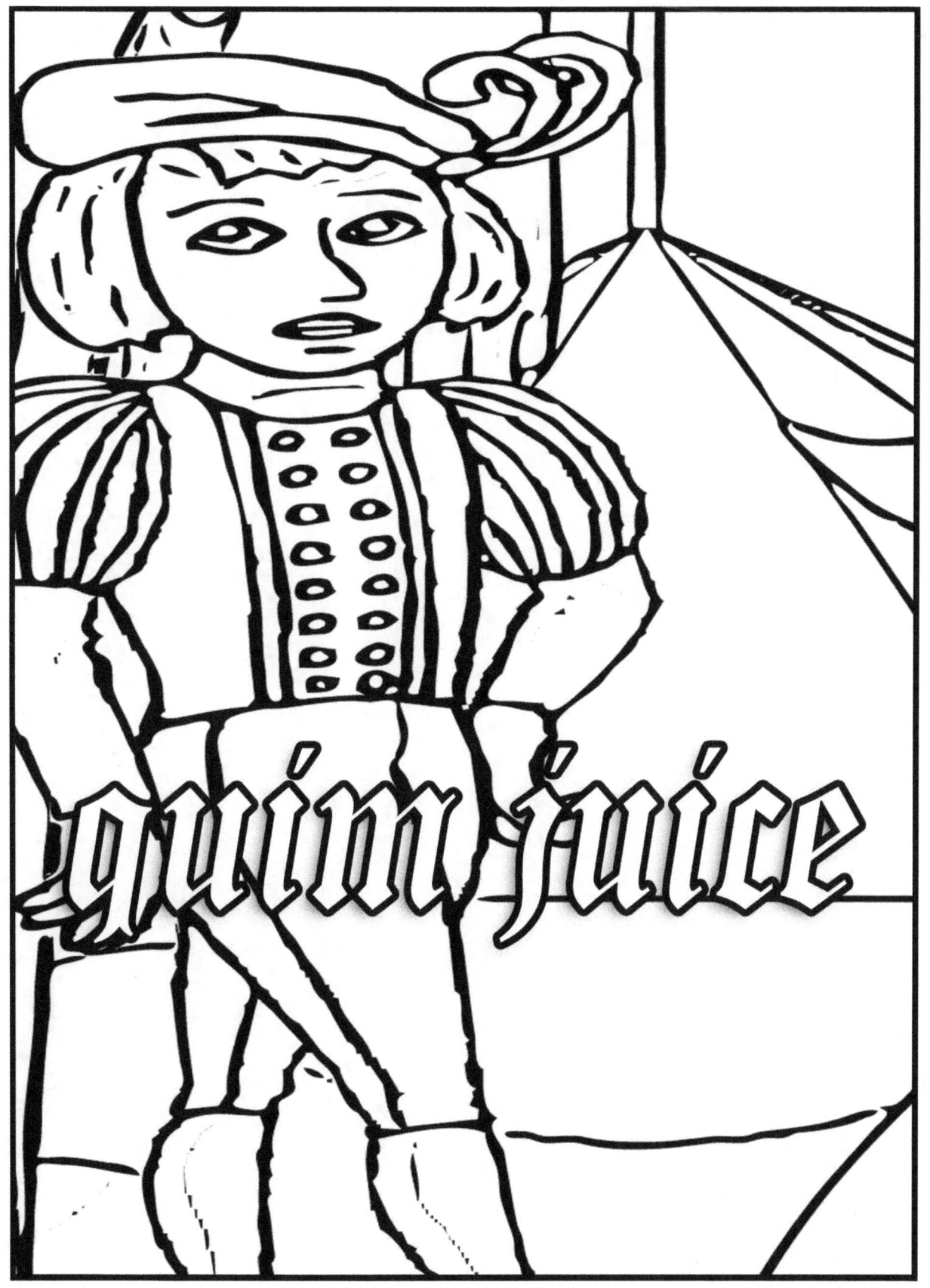

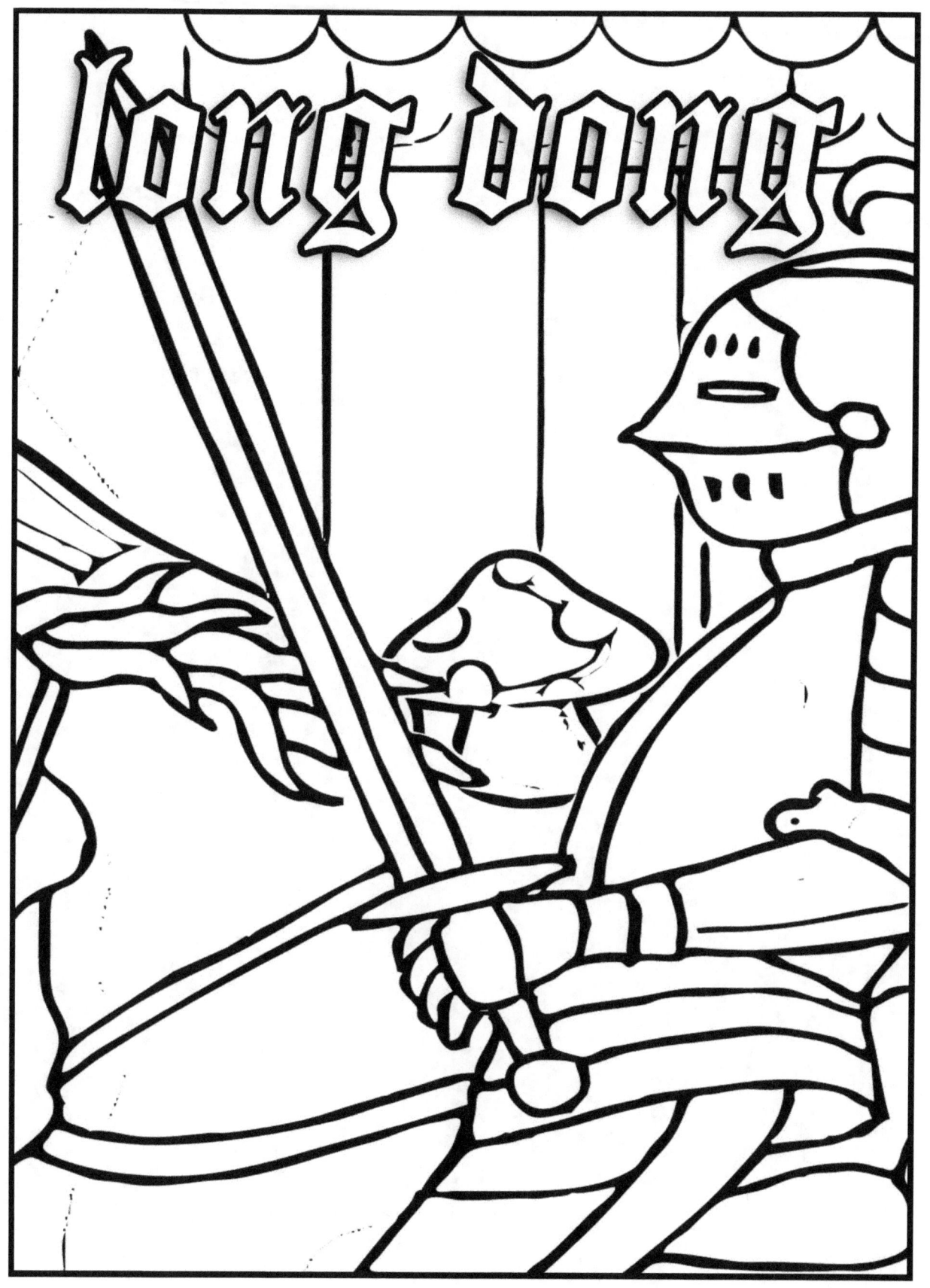

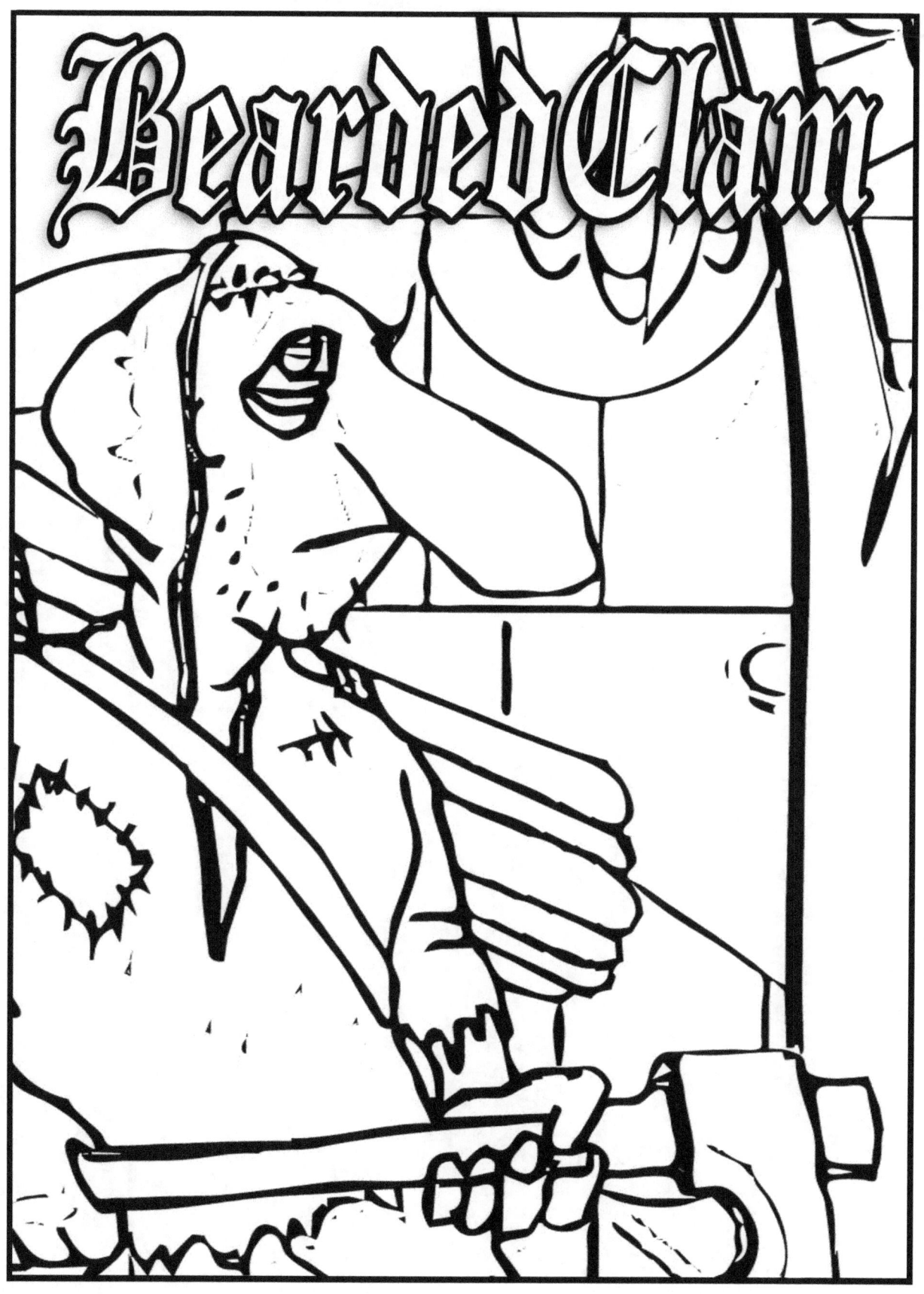

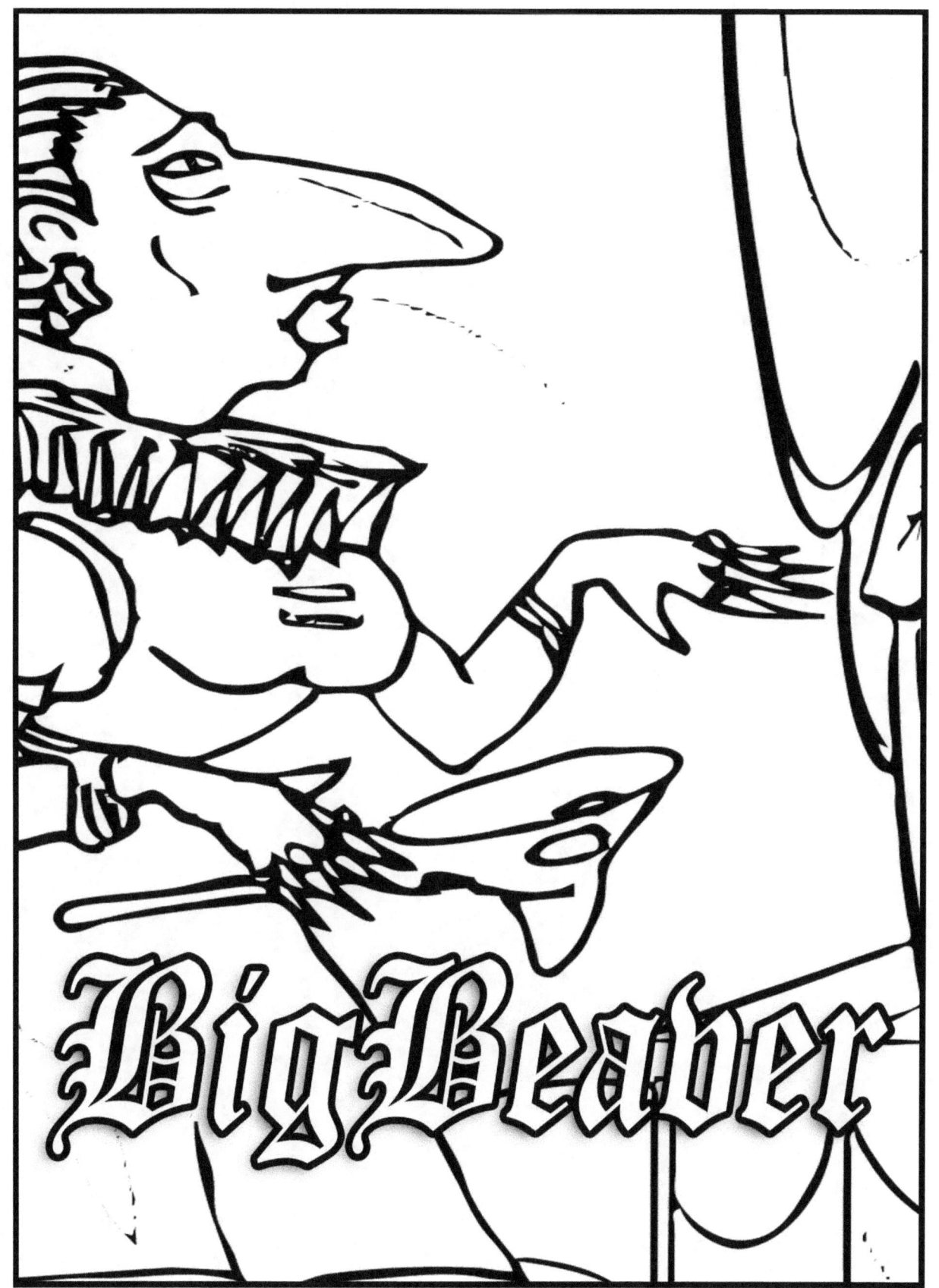

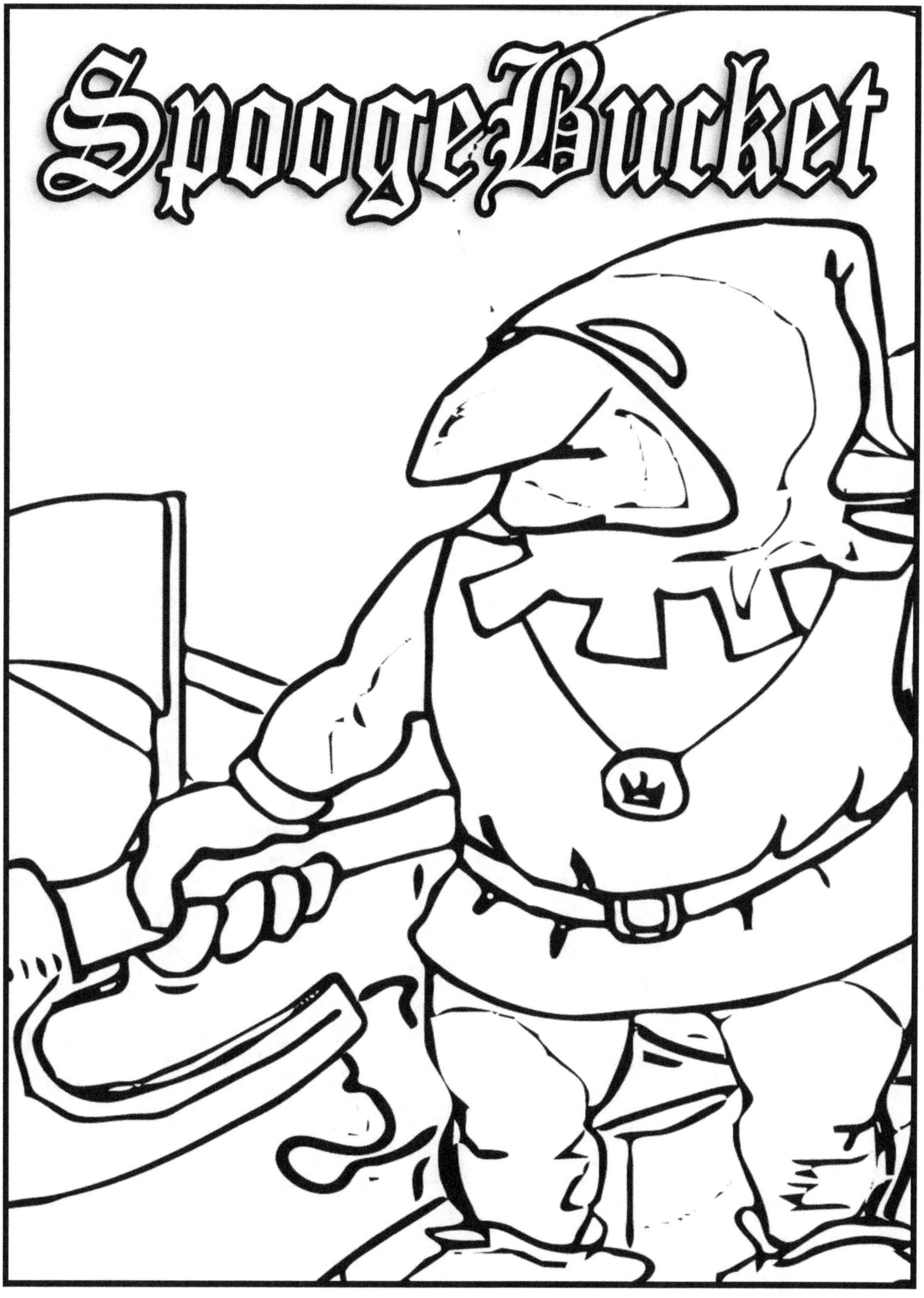
SpoogeBucket

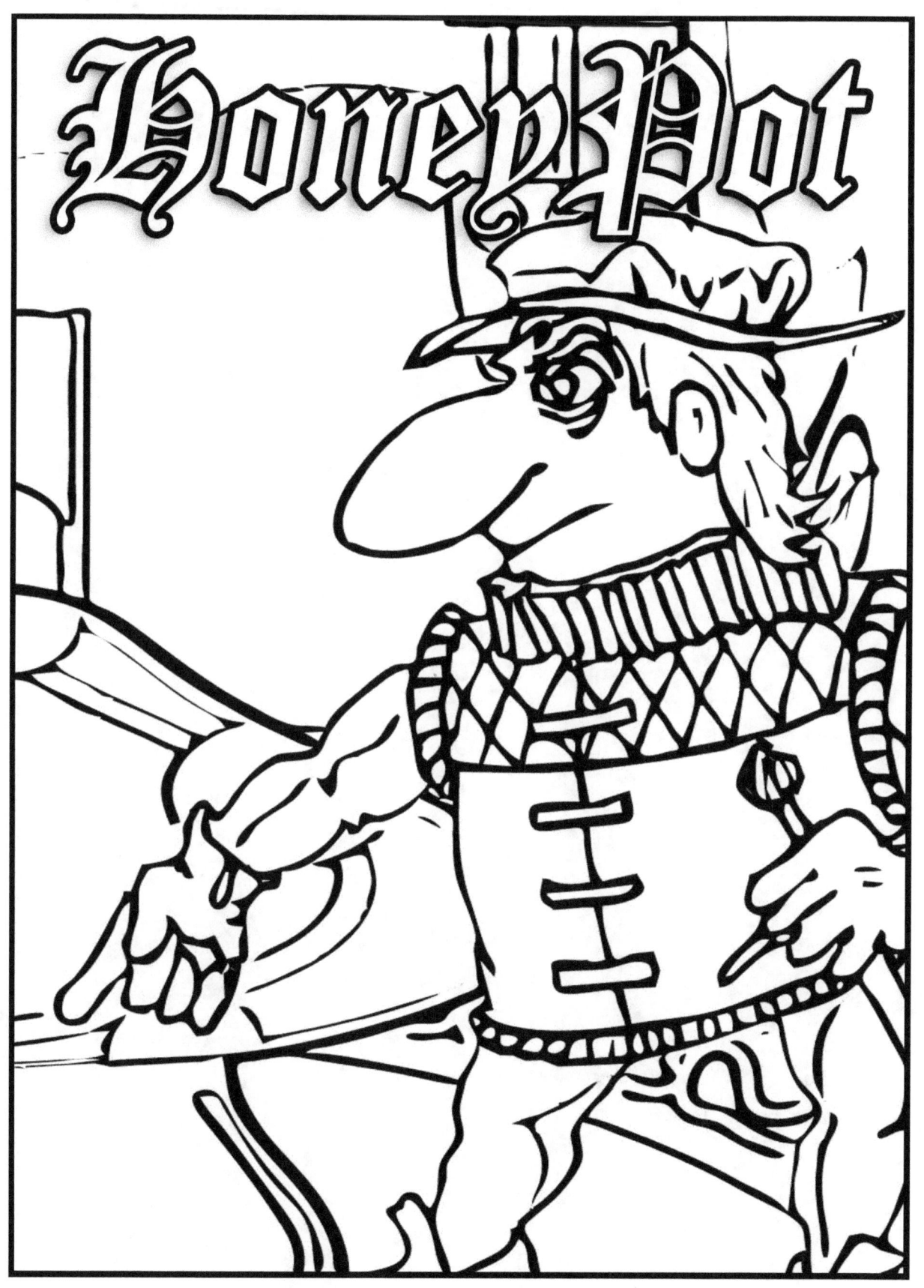

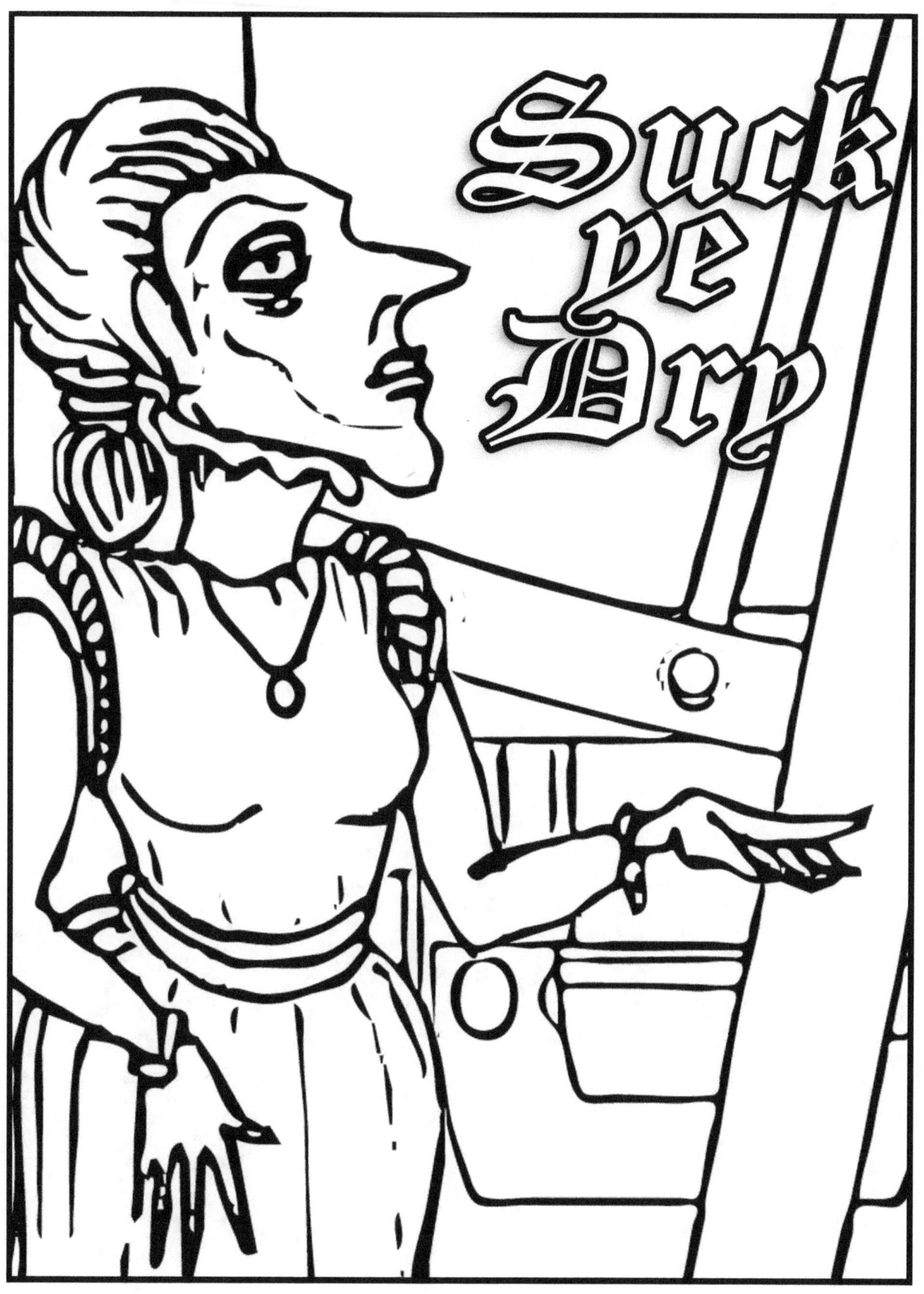

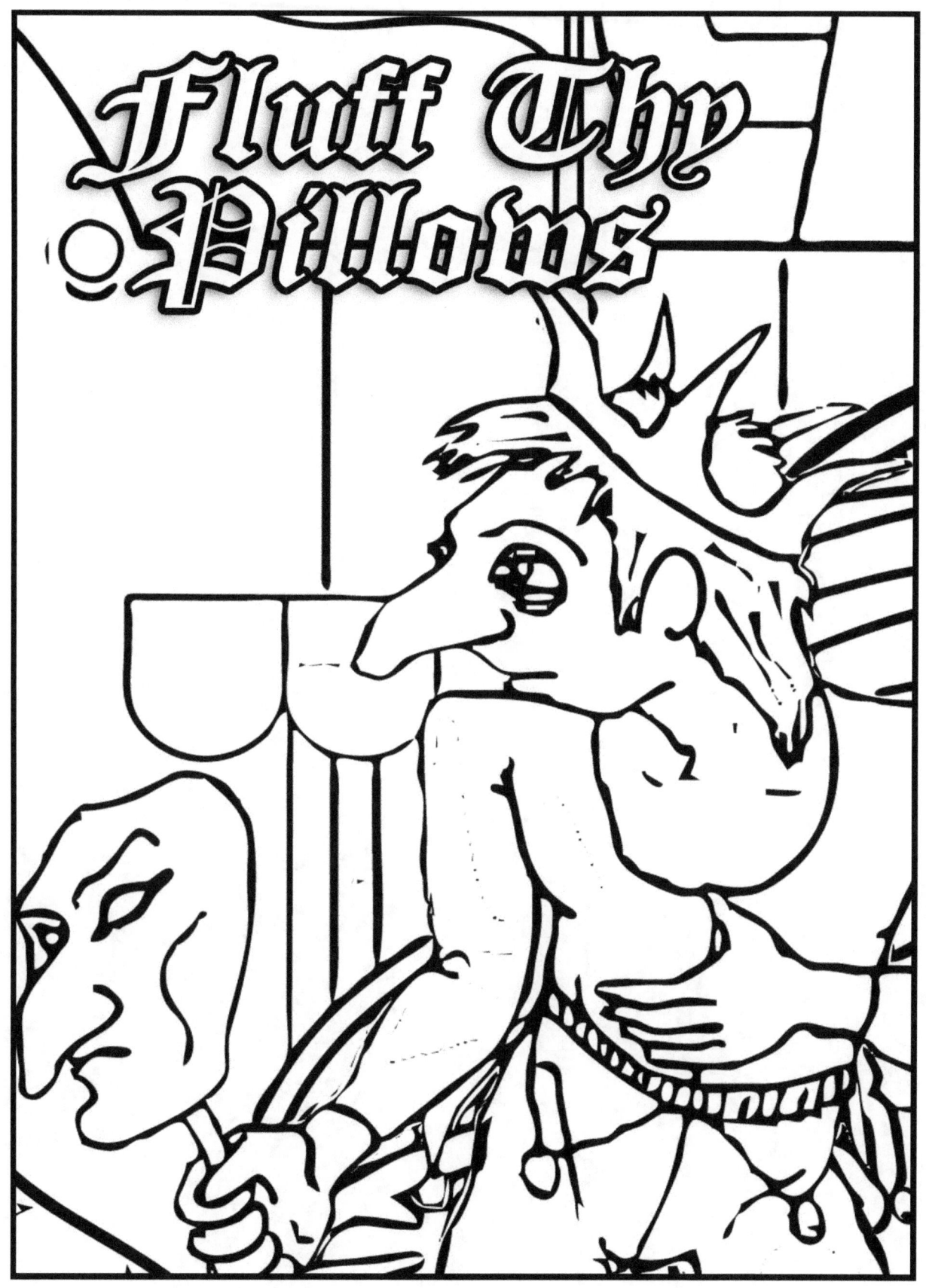

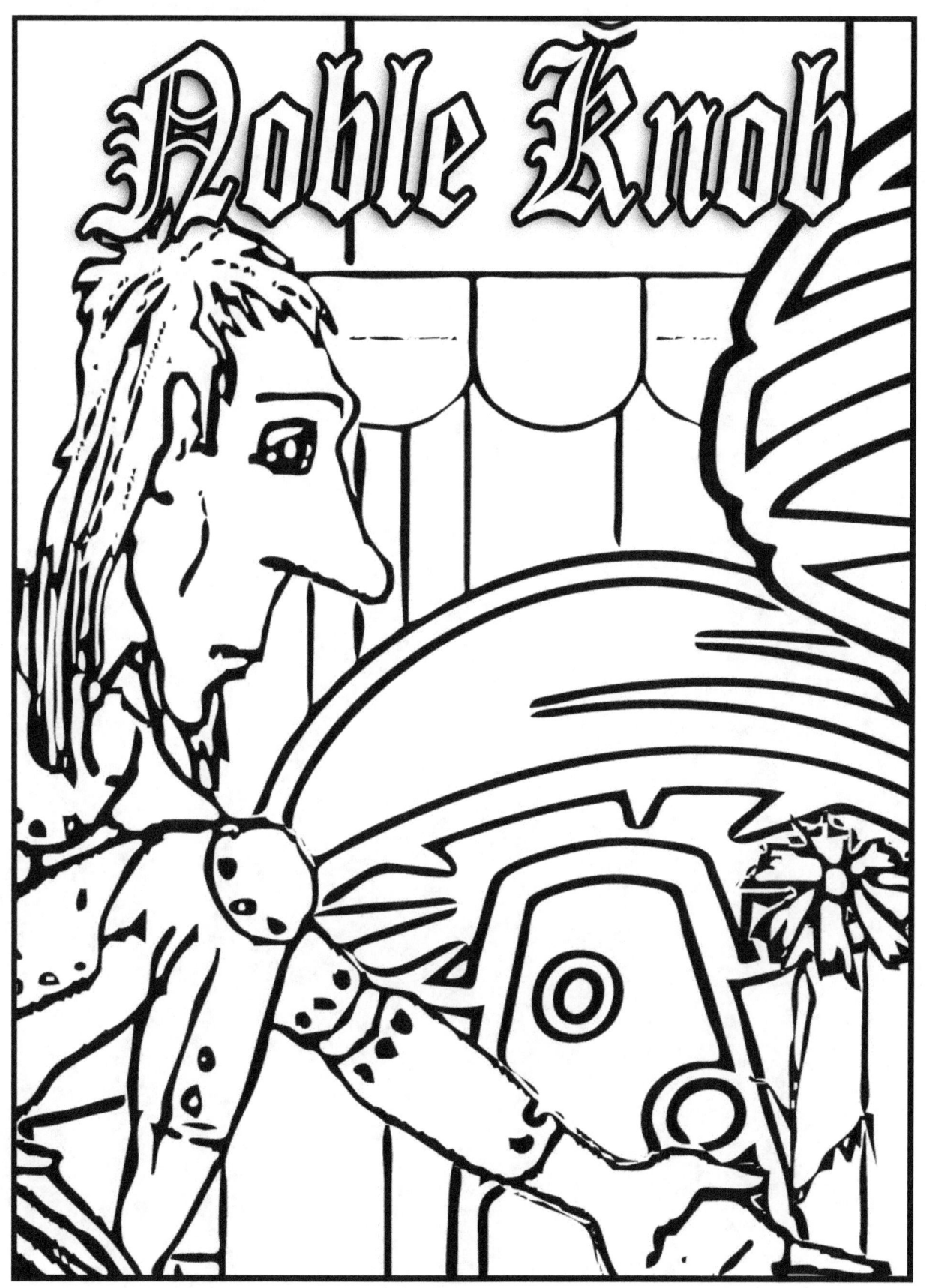

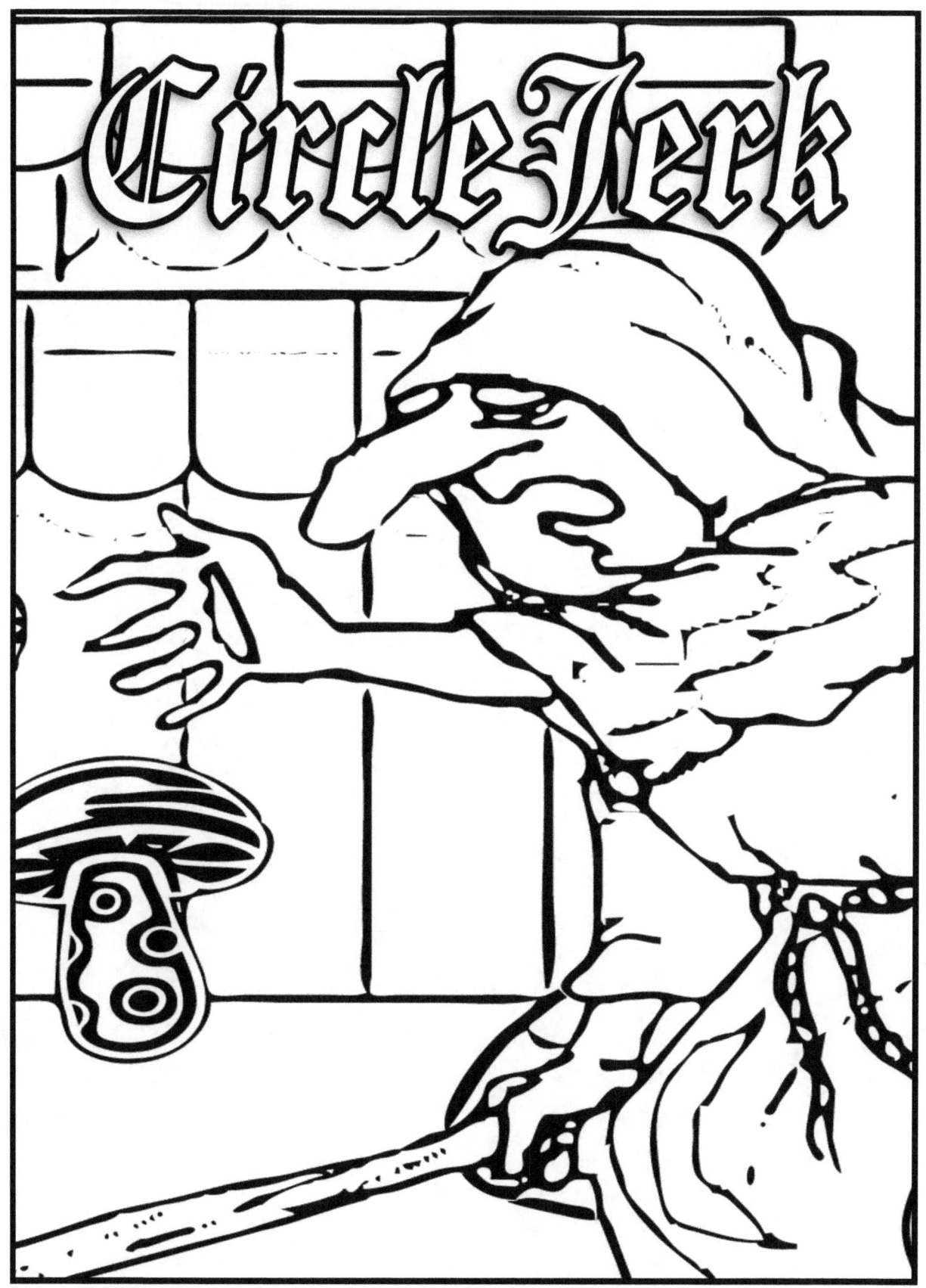

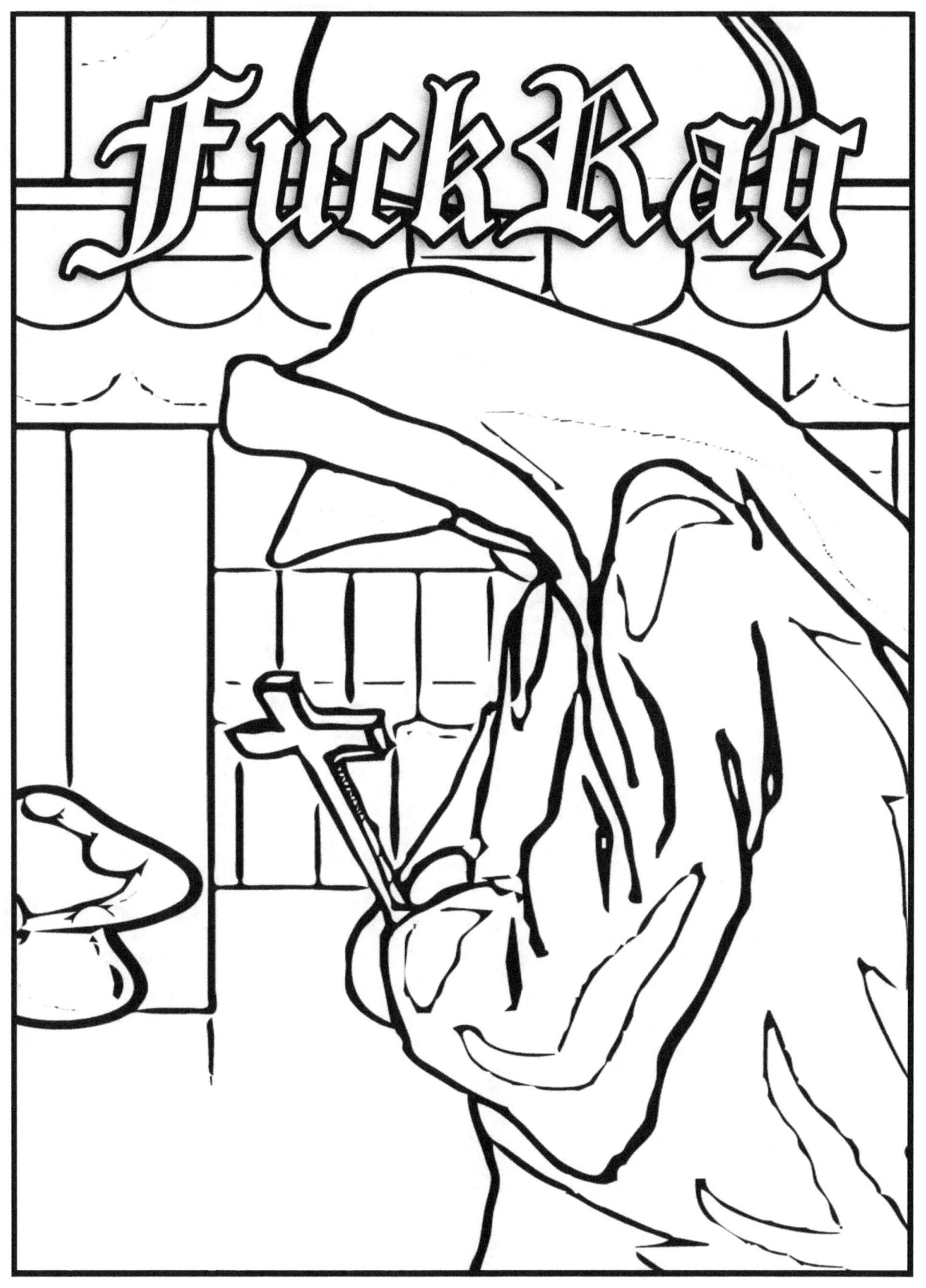

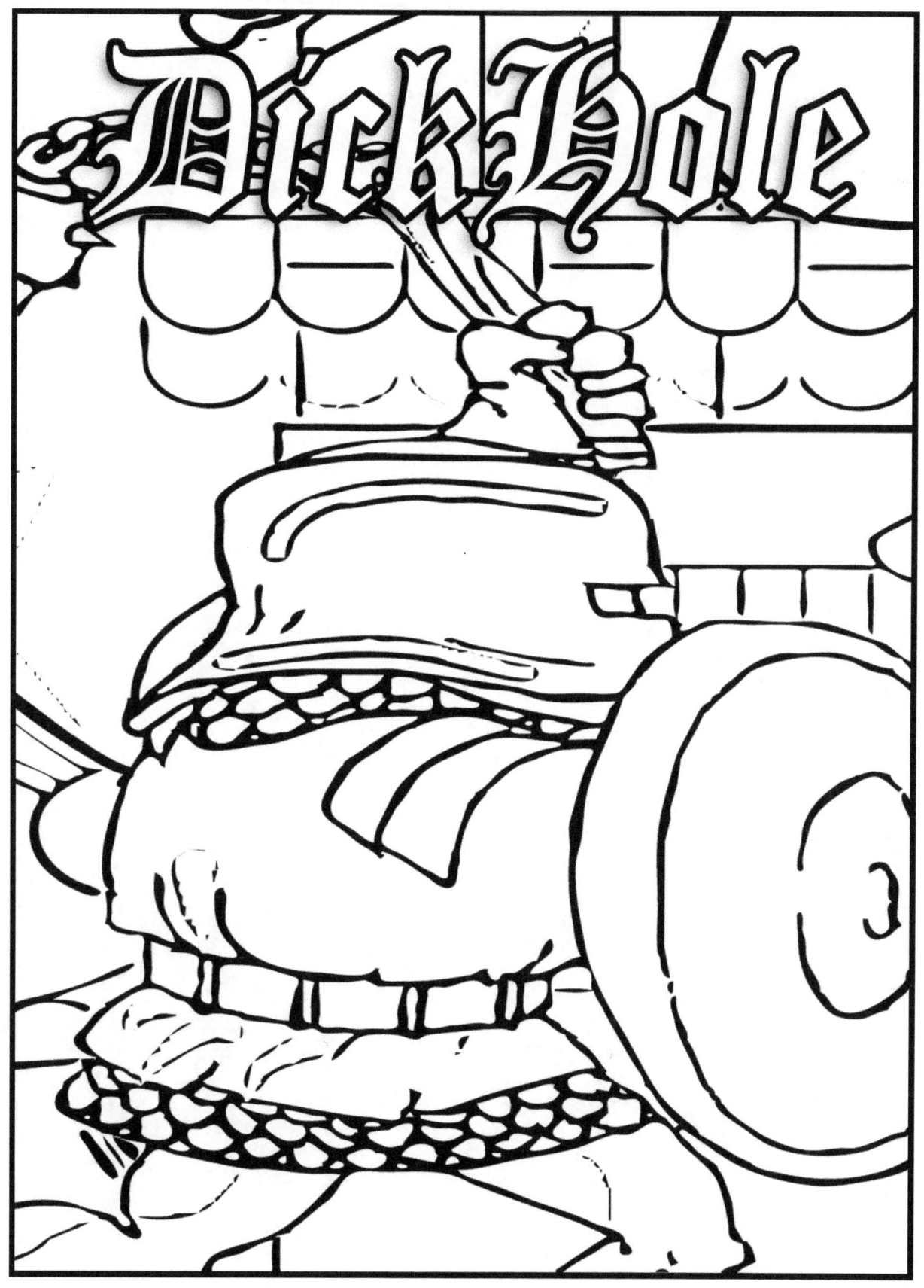

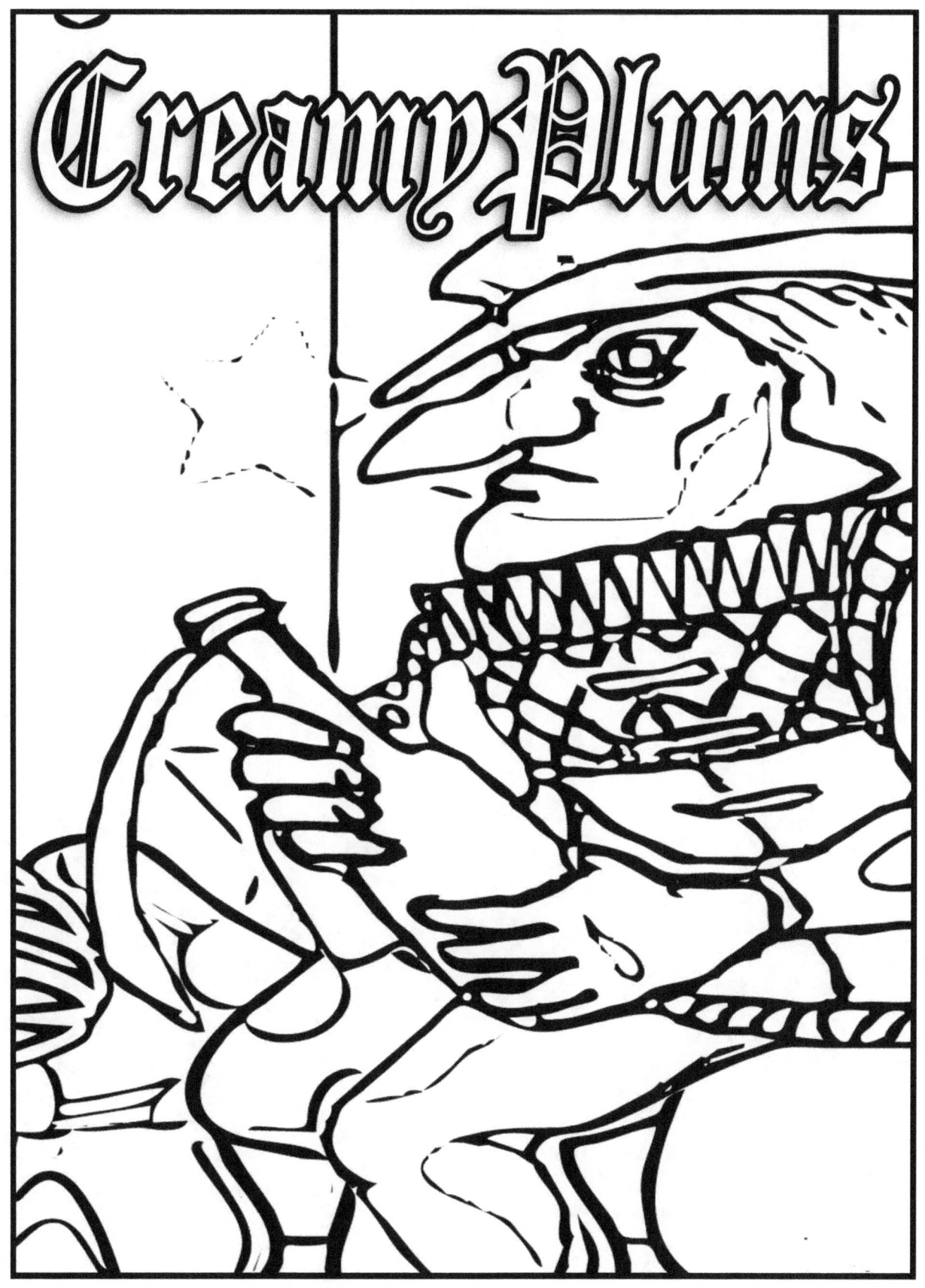

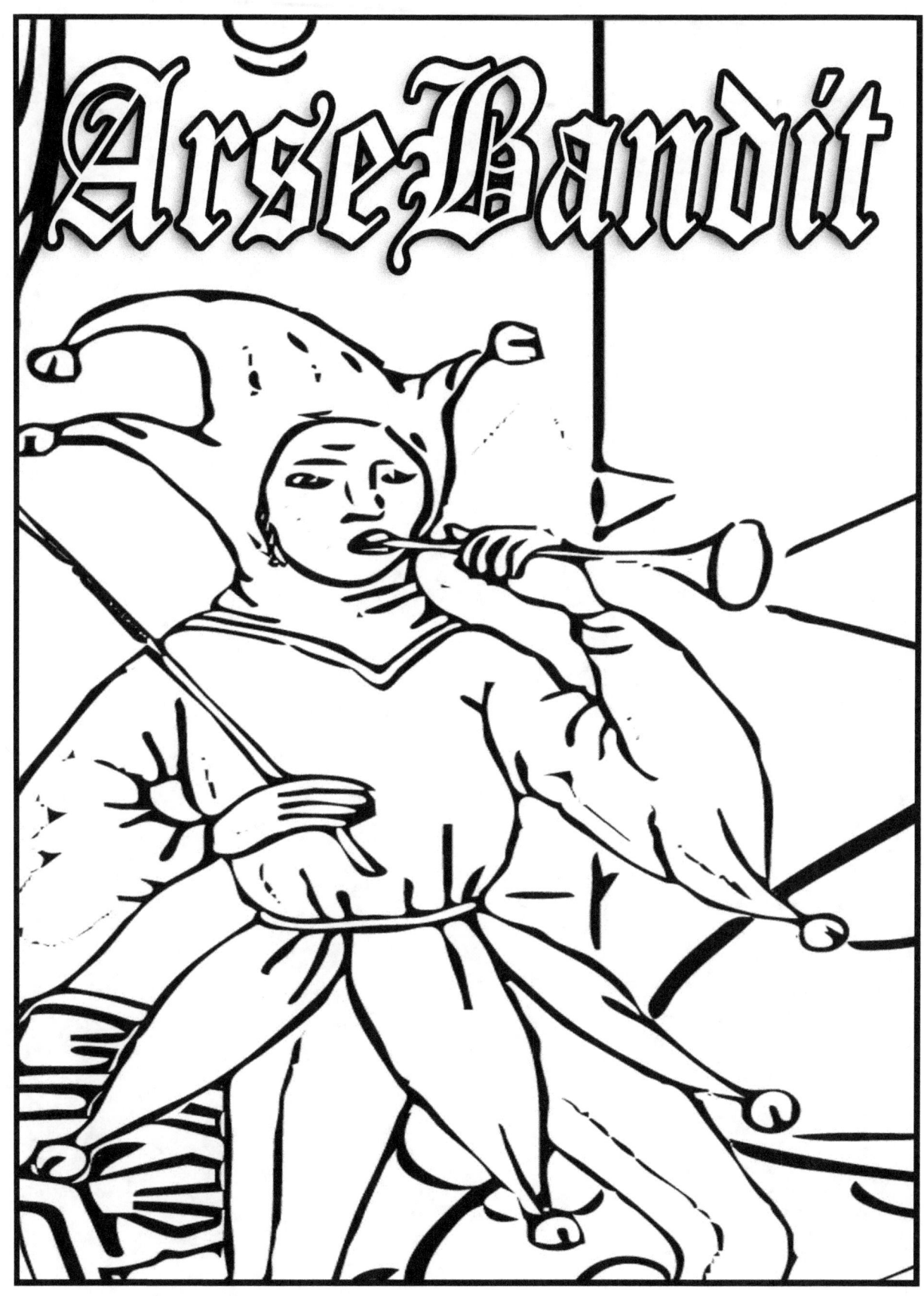

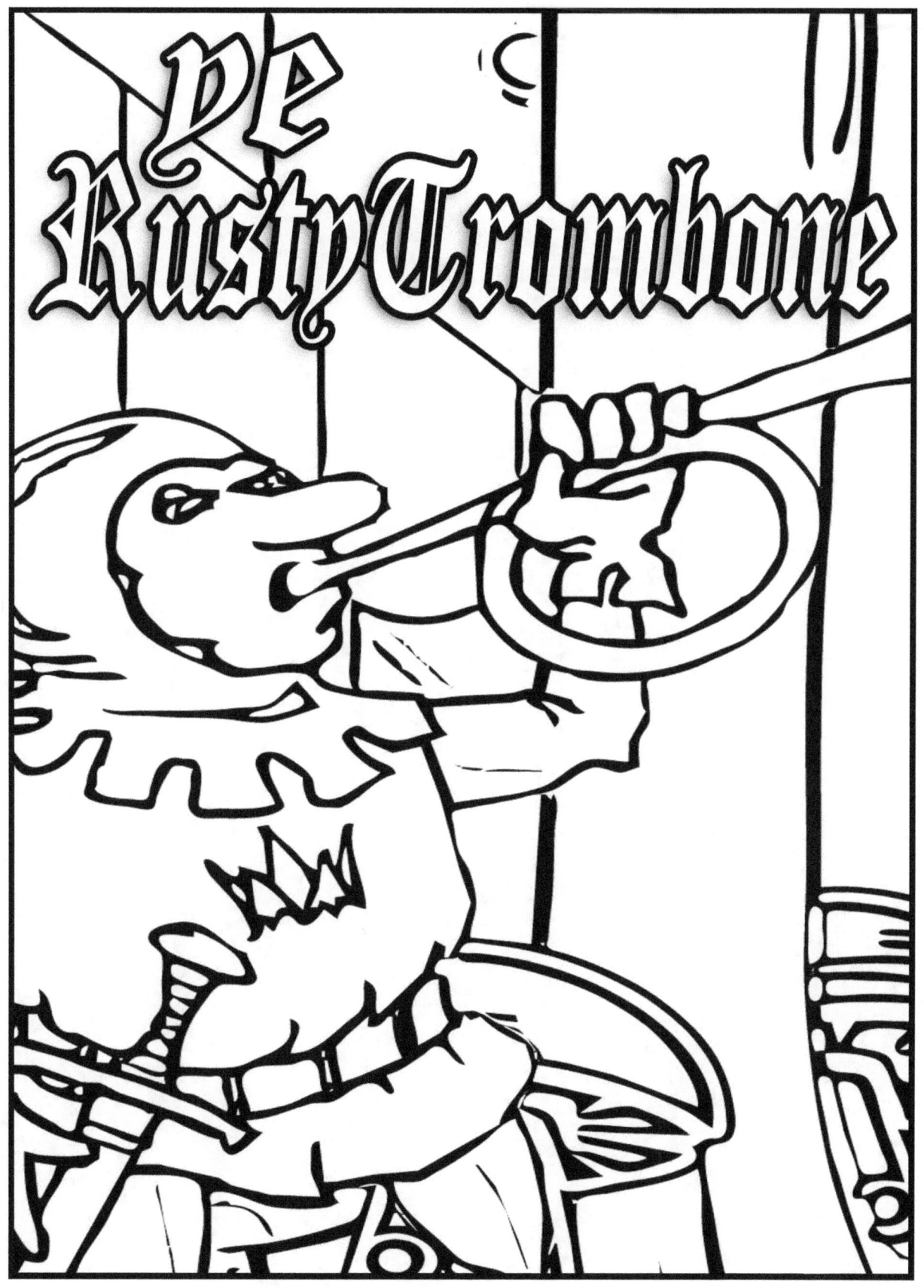

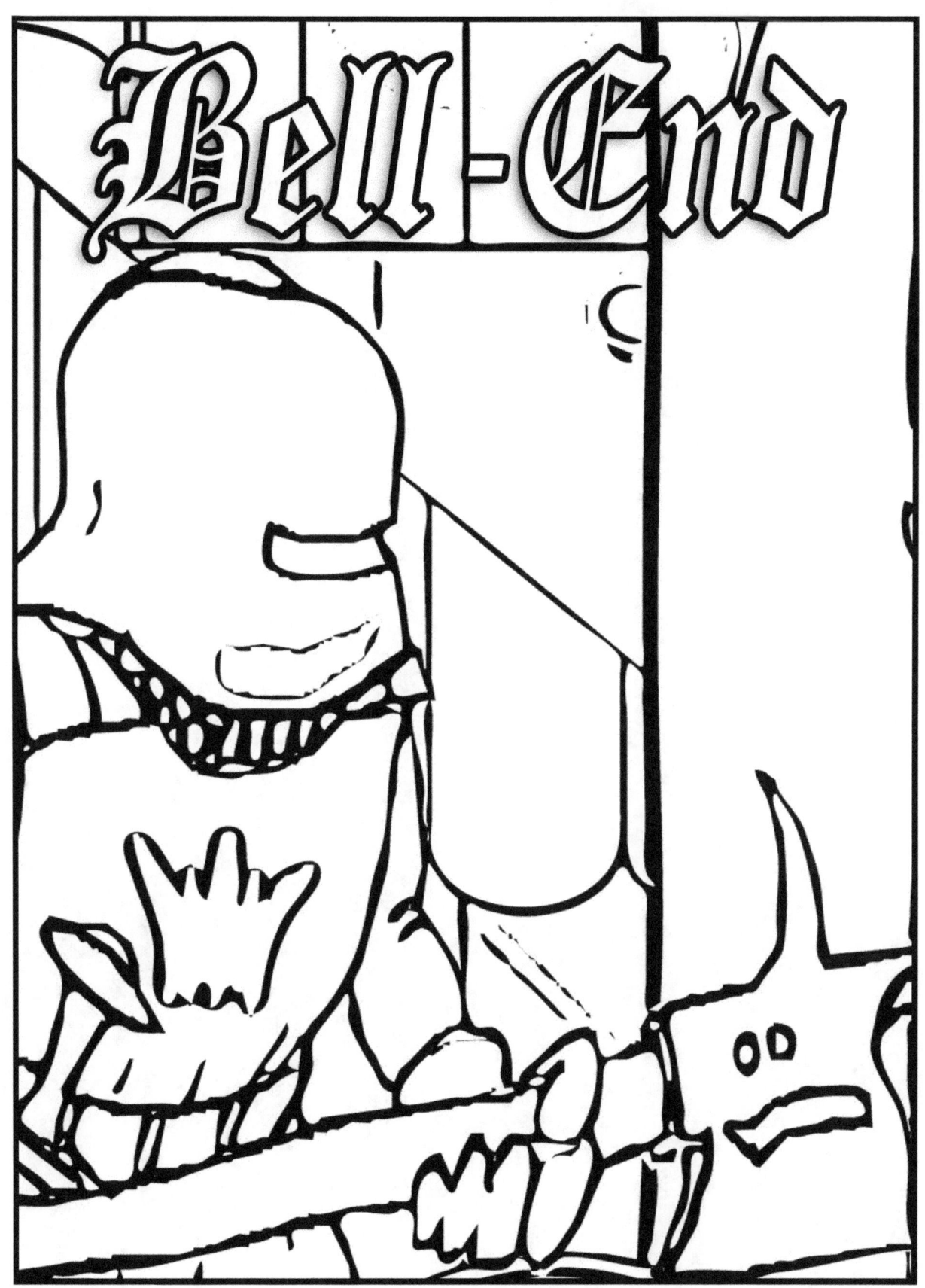

www.ingramcontent.com/pod-product-compliance
Lightning Source LLC
Chambersburg PA
CBHW080526190526
45169CB00008B/3064